# 10
## Prescriptions
## for a
## Healthy
## Church

# 10 Prescriptions for a Healthy Church

# WORKBOOK

## Bob Farr
## Kay Kotan

Abingdon Press™

*Nashville*

TEN PRESCRIPTIONS FOR A HEALTHY CHURCH
WORKBOOK
*Copyright© 2015 by Abingdon Press*

All rights reserved.

*This book is printed on acid-free paper.*

ISBN 978-1-63088-575-5

All scripture quotations unless noted otherwise are taken from the Common Engilsh Bible. Copyright © 2011 by the Common English Bible. All rights reserved. Used by permission. www.CommonEnglishBible.com..

The readiness test on pp. 5–6 is from *The Complete Ministry Audit*, Second Edition, pp. 36–37, by Bill Easum with Robert Brydia (0-687-49750-7), and is used by permission from Abingdon Press. Copyright © 2006. All rights reserved.

15 16 17 18 19 20 21 22 23 24—10 9 8 7 6 5 4 3 2 1
MANUFACTURED IN THE UNITED STATES OF AMERICA

# Contents

# Introduction

This workbook is a guide to the process of self-evaluation or consultation for a congregation. It is a companion to the book of the same title. If you are skipping right to the workbook, you are doing yourself and your church a great disservice. Take the time to read the book with other leaders of the church. Talk about it. Pray about it. Then, if you decide to move forward, gather the leaders of your church together and start the process of completing this workbook. Be sure to complete each section before moving along to the next. This is a process where one step builds on the next. Without taking each step in order, you are likely to not have the outcome you hope and pray for.

At the end of each chapter, you will find discussion questions and a checklist. The discussion questions are designed to help you and your team work through some of the details and planning. Take the time to answer these questions together with the appropriate teams (indicated in the questions) to ensure you are not missing any details or steps. There are lots of moving parts in this transformation process. This is our attempt at helping you manage all the parts! The checklist at the end of each chapter is a quick overview of the steps to complete in that particular phase of the process. It serves as both a summary and a place for you to literally check off the task when completed. There are some folks that receive great joy and a sense of accomplishment in being able to mark a task as completed.

Remember—this is a slow process. If you rush the process, it can be detrimental to the church for years if not decades to come. Be patient. Allow the Holy Spirit to be a part of it. Be methodical. Slowly and personally invite others along the way to be a part of this transformation process. For when our hearts are pure in intention, God blesses our good works. May you and your church be blessed in this journey of transformation for the glory of God.

# Section One
# Continuous Learning Groups

As you learned in our companion book, the way we must "do" church in the twenty-first century is not the same way we've done church in the past. We must learn the "what and why" of doing church differently. We must understand how our culture around us has changed. We must understand how our world has changed. We need to spend time understanding how effective, compelling churches are doing church today that is relevant and contextual for reaching new people. In order to accomplish all of this, we must spend some time learning. Learning is best experienced in a mixture of personal learning along with group learning. For that reason, we recommend using our lay leadership development materials, which can be found under the Resources tab on www.HealthyChurchInitiative.org.

Gather your pastor and a team of leaders (a group of eight to twelve) to form a continuous learning community. This team will then spend about eight months going through the lay leadership development materials. The members of the continuous learning community read the books on their own, and then the team gathers together to discuss their learnings from the books and to apply them to their church. An action step is created each session, so not only is learning happening, but you are also applying your learning.

As a best practice, the team of leaders working through the lay leadership development materials would then each invite eight to twelve people into a small group and study the same materials with them. This is to multiply the learning and bring more people into the conversation. Through the learning materials, the church will develop a new way of looking at the church of today and even create a new vocabulary.

You are welcome to mix and match the different sections of the various learning community materials on our website. Don't feel you need to do them exactly as they are printed. Along the way, we have contextually modified them. Just make sure you are hitting all the main categories rather than repeating the same categories. The

1

learning is designed to create conversation and a new awareness of the purpose of the church and how to go about becoming a church with the mission of "making disciples of Jesus Christ for the transformation of the world."

If the first round of learning communities creates a sense of energy and momentum to try a next step, then gather your leaders to discuss a possible consultation. If the learning didn't quite create a sense of energy and momentum, then try another round of different materials or different people in learning communities. Sometimes churches have two or three rounds of learning communities before they are ready for the next step. That is okay! You are much better off spending more time in this step and making sure your church is ready than moving too quickly to the next step and finding out you don't have enough people on board to make it all happen.

Creating the learning communities is recommended for two reasons. The first is covered above. That first reason is to learn the how, why, and what we must do to be a compelling, contextually relevant church tomorrow and in the decades to come. The second reason is to create a new culture. The new culture is one of continuous learning. Our world is changing; it always has been. Yet, our world is changing at a much faster pace than ever before. We must be continually studying and learning about the culture we live in to make sure we know how to reach it for Christ. If we sit back and watch the world around us change and we don't change as a church, we will become irrelevant, decline, and not accomplish our mission of making disciples. So please understand what you are creating here. This is not just about eight sessions of learning; this is about creating a culture of continuous learning.

# Section 1 Discussion Questions

## *Team Recruitment*

Who are the people that would be included in the learning community? What would you be looking for in those being recruited? Mature, committed Christians? Folks eager to learn and open to change? A new generation of leaders? A multigenerational mix to create rich conversation?

First make a list of the qualities you are seeking. Next make a list of those you would like to invite to be a part of the learning community.

## *Team Expectations*

What commitment are you asking of those recruits for the learning community? How much time (each session, how many sessions, outside the group) are you asking for? What are your expectations for them in regard to reading and studying? Prayer? Leading a group later? Attendance? Others?

List below the expectations so you will be ready to clearly articulate these to those you invite into the learning community.

## *Resource Selection*

What resources will your learning community use? Who will check out the resources and make recommendations? When will the materials be chosen and ready for the group's use?

Describe below the process you will use to choose the materials, who is taking responsibility for choosing them, and when the materials will be selected.

## *Sharing and Communication*

With which groups in your church do the learnings of the community need to be shared? How will this happen? Who will do the sharing? When? What is the purpose of the sharing?

Below first describe why the communication is important and what the message will be. Second, begin to make a list of groups to share with, who will share, and when they will share.

## *Readiness*

How will you decide if your church is ready to move ahead to section 2? Who needs to be a part of that discussion? Who needs to be a part of that decision?

Describe below what you would need to see in the life of the congregation to know the church is prepared to move ahead. Next describe who would need to be part of that discussion and decision. A readiness test is provided that could be utilized in this evaluation process.

## *Readiness Test*

Decide how you feel about the following statements and circle the appropriate number under each statement. Rate yourself on a scale of one to ten. One means that you totally agree with the statement. Ten means that you totally disagree with the statement and have no desire to change your attitude.

**Agree**                              **Neutral**                              **Disagree**

1. The nursery should be extra clean and neat, staffed with paid help, and open every time there is a church function.

1        2        3        4        5        6        7        8        9        10

2. Turf issues are harmful to the growth of a church.

1        2        3        4        5        6        7        8        9        10

3. I am willing for the facilities to be used even if they might get dirty.

1        2        3        4        5        6        7        8        9        10

4. Reaching out to new members is just as important as taking care of the present members.

1        2        3        4        5        6        7        8        9        10

5. I am comfortable with radical change if it will help my church reach more people for Christ.

1        2        3        4        5        6        7        8        9        10

6. I am seldom concerned about procedure.

1        2        3        4        5        6        7        8        9        10

7. Praying off the debt is not a major concern for me.

1        2        3        4        5        6        7        8        9        10

8. I support the idea of spending some of the church's savings in order to hire more staff or start new programs/ministries.

1        2        3        4        5        6        7        8        9        10

9. Several worship services are fine with me because I am more interested in meeting the needs of all the people than I am in knowing everyone at church.

1        2        3        4        5        6        7        8        9        10

10. I am not at all offended when my pastor does not give me regular, personal attention.

1        2        3        4        5        6        7        8        9        10

11. I realize that more staff are needed today than in the past.

1        2        3        4        5        6        7        8        9        10

12. I always trust and affirm my pastor's efforts to reach more people for Christ.

1        2        3        4        5        6        7        8        9        10

# Section 1 Checklist

_____ Gather a group of leaders to commit to learn together.

_____ Gather the lay leadership development materials and books.

_____ Meet together for a minimum of eight sessions.

_____ Learn, discuss, pray, apply, and take small action steps.

_____ Talk to others about what you are learning.

_____ Decide if your church is ready to move ahead. If so, proceed to section 2. If not, create more continuous learning groups. Spend time together learning, praying, applying, and taking action steps.

# Section Two
# Team Preparation

This section is designed to take you to the second stage on your journey of church transformation once you have completed section 1 and are ready for what is next. Section 2 encompasses four different steps:

1. Prayer team

2. Vision team

3. Completion of the self-study

4. Contract with Faith Perceptions for mystery worshippers

## Prayer Team

This step cannot be overly emphasized. I repeat, this step cannot be overly emphasized. For a transformation process to be effective, it must be bathed in and undergirded in prayer. Many churches already have prayer teams. However, my guess is there is a good chance that the type of prayer team that is needed for a transformation process does not exist. We are asking your church to put together a prayer team with an outward focus. Many times existing church prayer teams are very inwardly focused. Their prayers center on the joys and concerns of the existing congregants. Assemble a prayer team of four to six people who are prayer warriors—those that are faithful to their prayer life and believe in the power of prayer. This prayer team will focus on prayer for the following:

- Those in the mission field that don't have a relationship with Christ (most likely at least 70 percent of your community)

- Your community leaders by name (e.g., mayor, city council members, police chief, fire chief, superintendents, principals, community service leaders)

- The transformation process (the congregation's openness to the process, the effectiveness and fruitfulness of the process, and so on)

- God's guidance and blessing on the transformation process

- Your pastor and leaders leading the process

- Guests by name who have attended church services or any other church event

The prayer team will be assembled and will gather weekly indefinitely. The team will also be asked to include these specific prayer points in their daily prayer life.

For inspiration, watch "HCI Prayer Team Harrisonville" on YouTube (https://www.youtube.com/watch?v=gk77jR2pjcw).

If your church is unable to recruit, assemble, and implement the duties of the prayer team, you are not yet ready for a transformation process. Prayer is a must. Prayer is not negotiable. Prayer is the foundation of the entire transformation process. Don't skip this critical step!

# Vision Team

After the prayer team is functioning, the next step is to assemble six to eight people to serve on the vision team. This team has multiple functions. Those functions include the following:

- Commitment to the church transformation process (understanding the why, what, and how)

- Assisting in compiling the church self-study

- Communication with the church to prepare them for the transformation process

- Conversations in large groups, small groups, and individually to bring people along

- Assisting the pastor in helping others dream about a fruitful future

The vision team is a critical part of the transformation process. Without a vision team, it is difficult for a pastor to gain and retain momentum first for openness to transformation and then for implementing transformation. This must be a lay-led movement. Without the support and active participation of the laity, the process will soon run out of steam, and when the pastor moves on to a different ministry, the transformation will not be sustained because it was the "pastor's" agenda rather than a congregational movement. This is why it is so critical to have a strong vision team that is committed to seeing the process through. Those recruited to the vision team will be sold out for the mission of making disciples and willing to potentially risk personal relationships in the church to do so. Not everyone will be on board, so the vision team is best made up of people who have unwavering support of the mission and are ready to make disciples! It is best if the vision team members have been involved in the continuous learning communities outlined in section 1. If they have, they fully understand the why, what, and how of church transformation.

In order to fully understand our current reality, the vision team will conduct a self-study. The vision team will be responsible for the preparation of this document. The vision team can certainly farm out pieces of the self-study for others not on the team to complete. But, ultimately the vision team is responsible for the end product. Later in this section, we will cover the self-study in detail.

One of the most important responsibilities of the vision team is to communicate with the congregation. This communication will be in a variety of fashions. This could include written forms of communication such as newsletter articles, bulletin inserts, e-mail blasts, and social media posts. The communication will also include sharing a new vision with the congregation, small groups, and individuals. This is a continuous and ongoing process to answer questions, continually cast a vision to do something new to reach new people, and be faithful to God to make disciples. Again, this communication is in coordination with and in support of the pastor. There must be a common, consistent vision and language with both the pastor and the vision team.

# Completion of the Self-Study

The third step in this section is the completion of a congregational self-study. The purpose of this self-study is for the pastor, leaders, and congregation to have a very clear picture of the current reality of the congregation. It is difficult to create a vision for the future without having a firm grasp on your currently reality. Some are in denial of the current reality. They are still living in the heydays of the 1960s and '70s. Some believe that if we just finally figure out the right programming, everything will return to those glory days. Some don't realize how the church has declined. It has most likely been a slow, steady decline so many don't fully grasp the current reality. So not only will the self-study give you historical perspective, it will also allow you to gain some current-day perspective about your community. Then the gaps of our history versus our community reality are more easily identifiable.

The self-study is no doubt very helpful for a consultation team. But, when the vision team shares the self-study and their insights from gathering and analyzing the information, it is also an extremely valuable tool for the congregation, too. In a three-inch binder containing the self-study, there is a snapshot of the history of the church (both things to celebrate as well as mourn) and a snapshot of the mission field as it is at the time of the self-study. When the vision team begins to talk about their findings in analyzing the information, it can start meaningful conversations in the church. It is a chance to celebrate the ministries. It is also a chance to see our opportunity for the future. So our learning here over the past decade is to use this as a tool for not only the consultation team but also the congregation. There are gems to be mined from it. There are jewels to use for effective communication to gain momentum for transformation.

Go to the HCI website and download a copy of the self-study.

# Mystery Worshippers

The last step in this section is to decide on whether you will contract with Faith Perceptions (or similar) for mystery worshippers. This is an important decision. While we think we can sometimes figure this piece out ourselves, we are often surprised at the results of the unchurched perceptions about our church. Remember, we likely have a blind eye to a guest's perspective. So it is difficult to walk in the shoes of a guest and provide valuable feedback and impressions. Having unbiased information from the unchurched is so valuable. We believe one of the keys to helping gain a clear understanding of how to reach new people is to hear from new people!

If you plan to proceed with mystery worshippers, you will want to contract with Faith Perceptions when you are beginning your self-study. The more time you give them, the more opportunity they will have to bring you a variety and number of mystery worshippers. Usually three months is minimum, but six months is a more reasonable time frame to allow for the mystery worshipper visits.

It is my (Kay's) recommendation to not tell the congregation about the vision team's decision to contract for mystery worshippers. If a congregation knows, they are usually putting on their "Sunday best" and the mystery worshipper will not have an authentic experience. Rather they will have an experience of people who are on guard and giving their best show. When we allow the mystery worshipper to see what we normally do on any given Sunday, we have the opportunity to learn the most from the experience.

# Readiness 360

We have used a couple of different tools to assess the readiness of a congregation for change and transformation. The tool we have found to be most helpful is Readiness 360. This tool is an online assessment for some of the members of your congregation to take. It is best for a cross section of your congregation to participate. Readiness 360 is a series of about sixty questions used to assess readiness in areas of spiritual intensity, missional alignment, cultural openness, and dynamic relationships. This tool is most helpful to assist in knowing how far and how fast the congregation can be pushed for transformation. It also identifies which areas are most likely to have pushback and which areas are most ripe for harvest.

# Section 2 Discussion Questions

## *Prayer Team*

Who will you gather for the prayer team? What are the expectations for this team? When will they gather? How often? What expectations would you have for the team members outside the group meetings (e.g., daily prayer)? How will you equip them for outwardly focused prayer? How will you help them understand the importance of prayer in the transformation process? Who will lead this prayer team?

First, write the expectations for a prayer team. Second, describe your expectations for a prayer team member outside of the group meetings. Third, begin to write down names of potential prayer team members to recruit.

## Vision Team

What expectations do you have for your vision team? These expectations could include time commitment, prayer commitment, studying materials outside the team, frequency the team gathers, and so on. What attributes would you be looking for in the team members? What will you do to equip this vision team? Who are some people you believe can meet your expectations and have the attributes that would lend themselves to being a part of the vision team?

First, describe the expectations for a vision team member. Second, describe the attributes you are searching for in vision team members. Third, describe the equipping process you will have for your vision team. Finally, write down some names of some people that God is placing on your heart that you would like to invite to be a part of the vision team.

# *Communication Plan*

How will you communicate to your congregation what your church is doing and, most importantly, why it is doing what it is doing? What needs to be communicated? Who needs to communicate? Who needs to hear it? When do they need to hear it? How do they need to hear it? How can you communicate in a variety of ways (sermon, newsletter, announcements, skits, small-group conversations, and so on)? At what frequency should the communication be completed?

Describe your communication plan below, making sure you include all the elements listed in the questions above. Next, list the various groups or people who need to hear and who will communicate with each group or person.

# *Congregational Self-Study*

When will the vision team start the self-study? When will it be completed? How will the work be divided? How will the contents and learnings from the self-study be shared with the congregation?

As a vision team, decide on the start and completion dates for the self-study. Using the self-study document from the HCI website as a guide, divide up the different sections of the self-study, and assign them to various vision team members. Below, record the beginning and end date for the self-study. Next, record the person responsible for each part of the self-study. Finally, describe the timing, process, and communication to be used for sharing the self-study with the congregation.

# *Faith Perceptions and Readiness 360*

Who from the vision team will contact Faith Perceptions and the folks responsible for Readiness 360? What spending authority does that person have to contract with these vendors? When do you want the mystery worshipper process to begin? Who are the people you would like to participate in the online Readiness 360 survey? When would you like them to take the survey?

Note below who is responsible to contact these two vendors as well as the budget for these services. Next, describe the type of folks you would like to complete the Readiness 360. Begin a list of those people you would like to invite to participate in the survey. Finally, list the timeframe in which you would like the survey to be completed.

# Section 2 Checklist

_____ Gather a group to commit to pray.

_____ Equip and support the prayer team for their work.

_____ Set the prayer team free to do their ministry (with ongoing support).

_____ Gather a group of leaders to commit to the vision team.

_____ Equip and support the vision team.

_____ Create a communication plan.

_____ Complete the congregational self-study.

_____ Contract with Faith Perceptions to bring in mystery worshippers.

_____ Contact Readiness 360 for an online assessment for congregants.

# Congregational Preparation

Once you have started the process, it is imperative to communicate, create momentum, and prepare the congregation for a transformation process. The time leading up to the weekend is just as important as the weekend itself. The more thorough the preparation, the more thorough and effective the outcome. Remember, this is a process, not a program. This process is about creating a new culture. It takes time. It takes bringing people along. It takes lots of prayer. It takes lots of patience. It takes lots of perseverance. It takes lots of bold and courageous leaders to be out in front of the congregation leading them to be faithful to being fruitful as a congregation.

This section will assist you with preparing your congregation for transformation to occur. It includes the following:

1. Creating urgency

2. Small group study

3. Continuing the prayer team

4. Preconsultation workshop

## Communication

You simply cannot overcommunicate about this process. You cannot talk about it too much. It is simply not possible. From the time the church decides to enter into this transformation process, the communication must begin, and it should, quite frankly, never end. If you are creating a culture of continuous transformation and evaluation to reach God's people in new and innovative methods, transformation and evaluation never end. We continuously look for ways to raise the bar of excellence. We continuously look for ways to be more competent and compelling. We continuously look for more and better ways to develop leaders, mature our disciples, and efficiently make kingdom decisions. This is *why* we must continuously talk about what we are doing and more importantly *why* we are doing it. People won't necessarily get excited about what you are doing until they know *why* you are doing it. The *why* is the big picture. The *why* is beyond us individually or us as a church. It is much bigger than either of those two things. The *why* is all about living out the Great Commission. The *why* is about maturing as disciples, where the focus becomes less about us and more about those that don't yet have a relationship with Christ. The *why* must be communicated before your congregation can grasp the what. Don't start communicating about the what until your congregation grasps the why.

Communication must take shape in many forms over a period of time. Communication needs to occur in worship in announcements, bulletin inserts, skits, drama, video clips, prayer, testimonials, and so on. Communication must also take the form of small group discussion. Have your leaders sit with the groups, teams, and committees in your church. Have them present on the why and what. Be open for questions. Be transparent in the exchange of information. Communication must also take place one on one. The leaders will want to engage their own social circle, key influencers, and those needing some extra help processing in conversation to help bring them along. Communication also needs to occur in newsletters, on Facebook, on the church website, on other social media, through e-mail blasts, and so on. Conduct town hall meetings with your congregation to give information and provide a time for people to ask questions. Engage in communication at every level possible and do it multiple times within each media.

Not everyone will be in favor of church transformation. Most likely people will be resistant to change because there is a real or perceived fear or loss. They may or may not be able to articulate their resistance to change and transformation. You can try to help bring them along with questions such as, "What frightens you about this?" or "What do you feel you might lose in this process?" Sometimes just helping them articulate why there is resistance is helpful. Sometimes no matter what you might say or do, they are just being resistant. Your job is not to bring consensus to the entire church to move forward. Your job is to give everyone the opportunity to be heard. Pray with and for these folks. Also know that you may lose a few people that are not on board for doing a new thing to reach new people. While this is not the intended outcome or desire of the process, it does happen from time to time. Let these people know you are sorry they won't be along for the journey, but you must move ahead with being faithful and fruitful to reach new people. You simply cannot be held hostage by people who cannot move in a new direction.

When you believe you have communicated enough, communicate some more. And when you think everyone has heard it a hundred times, you will be surprised when someone says they have no idea what is going on. Expect this, and communicate some more.

You will also want to be inviting people to participate in the dream weekend by attending the workshop, participating in the focus group, and being interviewed.

# Urgency, Sermon Series, and Small Groups

In order to create a sense of urgency for transformation, you must do so with intentionality. The month leading up to the consultation is a perfect time for this. This time of preparation is for the heart. All the head work of communication, self-study, assessment, mystery worshipers, and so on is now completed. Now is the time to prepare our hearts for what God is calling us to do and become as a congregation. One way to create this openness and urgency is to preach a four- to six-week sermon series of preparation and prayer. We suggest using resources such as *Remember the Future* by Bishop Robert Schnase or *Does Your Church Have a Prayer?* by Marc Brown, Kathy Merry, and John Briggs. Along with the sermon series, launch a four- to six-week small group study to accompany the sermon series. This will allow small groups to go deeper into the text. Ask each small group to be in prayer for the pastor, leaders, church, community, and process. Be in prayer that God will provide you with the vision to reach more people.

# Prayer Team

The prayer team continues meeting collectively and praying individually. They are praying for the unchurched, the community (mission field), the community leaders, the process, and any consultants or coaches you are bringing into the process. They are also praying for God's vision for the church to reach more people. The prayer team members could also be meeting with the small groups and praying with them. Remember, this process is most effective when it is wrapped, bathed, and undergirded in prayer.

# Preconsultation Workshop

On the HCI website, you will find a PowerPoint presentation and participant handout for a preconsultation workshop. This workshop is most commonly presented by either a coach or consultant who would be working on the consultation team for the consultation weekend. This is a best practice because it is an outside voice beginning to bring in an outside perspective that has no ties (relational, emotional, or supervision driven) to the congregation. By using an outside person, it begins the opportunity for there to be a truth teller in the conversation, that is, someone who can hold up the mirror and speak candidly about the current condition of the church, what best practices vital churches are using, and what God calls your church to be. However, a leader in the congregation could lead this workshop.

The content of the preconsultation workshop is designed to help people understand why transformation is needed. It is also designed to talk about the cultural changes in the secular world and how they relate to church culture. The workshop also introduces the life cycle of a church, why it is important to know about it, and the elements present or absent from each stage in the life cycle. This gives the church an opportunity to self-identify where they believe their church is at in the life cycle. The teaching about the life cycle gives the church another tool to identify the level of healthiness in their own congregation. The final component of the workshop is to talk about the five practices of fruitful congregations. Knowing these are the five best practices, the participants have an opportunity to assess how they believe the church is doing in each of the five practices.

The purpose of the workshop is to gain more awareness, create urgency, prepare the congregation, and start preliminary conversations and thoughts about transformation. This is also a great first step in building a relationship between a consultant or coach and your congregation.

# Section 3 Discussion Questions

## *Communication Plan*

You are continuing to build on the communication plan you created from the previous two chapters/phases (learning communities and team preparation) of the process. What further steps, people, methods need to be explored to best communicate? What is working well? What is not working well? Where are there gaps in communication? What is the vision team's strategy to fill those gaps?

Review and reflect upon the communication plans in the previous two chapters. Describe below what changes or additions need to be implemented in your communication plan and who is responsible for the implementation.

# *Sermon Series and Small Groups*

What sermon series and small-group experience will you offer the thirty days prior to your consultation weekend? Who is responsible for selecting the materials? How will the small groups be recruited and assembled? Who is responsible for the coordination of the small groups and their leaders? Who will equip the small-group leaders? How will the worship elements (liturgy, video, still images, music, prayer, chancel area decorations, props, bulletin, and so on) reflect the discernment process the church is experiencing?

Below indicate who is responsible for material selection and the due date for doing so. Next, indicate the person responsible for the small groups and when this recruitment process for both the leaders and groups will begin. Finally, describe who is responsible (e.g., the worship design team) for creating a worship experience that fully reflects the discernment process, sermon series, and small-group experience.

# *Preconsultation Workshop*

Who will your church bring in to conduct the preconsultation workshop? When will the workshop be conducted? How will the congregation be invited and encouraged to attend?

Name below who will be conducting your preconsultation workshop. If this person needs to be contacted, note who is responsible for contacting them and what the budget is for bringing this person in. Set the time and date for the preconsultation workshop, and write it below. Next, describe the process and who is responsible for inviting and encouraging the congregation to attend.

# *Interviews and Focus Group*

Who is responsible for putting together the interview schedule, sending invitations, and confirming participation? Who is responsible for inviting and confirming the focus group participants? Who needs to be interviewed? Who do you want in the focus group? When does the recruitment for both of these groups need to begin?

Note below who is responsible for the interviews and who is responsible for the focus group. Next, begin to list the people who will be invited to participate in each group. Finally, determine the date for the recruitment to begin.

# Section 3 Checklist

\_\_\_\_\_ Prepare and implement a plan for communication.

\_\_\_\_\_ Create a sermon series to prepare to hear God's work for the church and create urgency.

\_\_\_\_\_ Launch a small group study to coordinate with the sermon series.

\_\_\_\_\_ The prayer team continues their work and brings others in the congregation along in prayer.

\_\_\_\_\_ Conduct a preconsultation workshop (best if done by an outside coach or consultant).

\_\_\_\_\_ Continue to refer to this is a process not a program.

\_\_\_\_\_ Set up interview schedule for Dream Weekend (see section 4 for details).

\_\_\_\_\_ Recruit the focus group.

Section Four
# Dream Weekend

## Best Practice: Outside Help

You have now reached the critical stage of your decision of whether to bring in outside help. As a best practice, the Dream Weekend process should be heard and facilitated by an outside person or team that is familiar with facilitating and leading church transformation. While the congregation will incur expenses for this to happen, it is an investment into the life of the congregation that can pay huge dividends. An outside voice, perspective, ears, and eyes can experience and reflect things to the congregation that those inside the congregation or closely related to the congregation can't recognize. An unbiased person without a stake in the church can be objective and see more of the current reality than those closely related to the situation. Someone from the outside can say and reflect the things that leaders and pastors are just not able to say to their congregations.

## Team Studies

The time leading up to the consultation is spent for preparation by both the congregation (see section 3) and the consultant, coach, or consultation team. There is a time to absorb the materials submitted in the self-study, the mystery worshipper report, and the Readiness 360 evaluation. This time to read, study, and absorb these materials is crucial before stepping into the Dream Weekend.

# THE DREAM WEEKEND BEGINS...

## *Interviews*

The Dream Weekend will begin with the consultation team interviewing the pastor, paid staff, leaders, and key influencers. This typically occurs on Friday. The first interview is with the pastor and lasts about ninety minutes. The rest of the day is spent with leaders, staff, and key influencers in thirty-minute conversations. The same set of questions is used for each leader. The pastor has the same questions plus several more. (See the HCI website for a set of questions.) After the first pastoral interview, the other interview slots are spaced forty-five minutes apart to give the consultation team time to process and take needed breaks between interviews. Typically, there are about eight interview slots throughout the day.

Depending on the size of your church, there may be a need for more interviewing time. If your church has a large staff or lots of leaders and key influencers that need to be heard, there may be a need to have two interview teams (made up of two people each). Another option is to start the interviews on Thursday rather than Friday so that there are two days of interviews rather than just one.

Friday also includes a facility tour so that the consultation team can experience the facility firsthand. The facility tour is typically led by the pastor as a part of their time with the consultation team.

## *Dinner with Pastor's Spouse*

After the conclusion of interviews on Friday (hopefully at about 5:00 p.m.), the consultant will take the pastor and spouse to dinner. The purpose of this is to allow the spouse to share his or her thoughts, dreams, hopes, and frustrations about the congregation. We also do this is a source of appreciation for the spouse's part in the ministry of the church. (See under the Resources tab on the HCI website for suggested questions for the spouse.)

## *Focus Group*

At approximately 7:00 p.m. on Friday evening, the consultation team will meet with a focus group. This is a group of people invited by the pastor to meet with the consultation team. (The pastor does not participate in the focus group.) The focus group is a cross section of the congregation. The participants are regular attenders but are not in current leadership roles. The focus group consists of each individual person responding to five questions. The focus group discussion is about ninety minutes long. See the HCI website for the interview questions.

The purpose of the focus group is to hear from regular attenders that are not in the same conversations as the leaders of the church. The consultation team is looking for similarities as well as differences in insights into the life of the congregation from these two perspectives.

## Meeting with the Leadership

On Saturday morning of the Dream Weekend, the consultation team will meet with the leaders (board/council) of your church. This will be a time of clarification, digging deeper, and questions. This is an opportunity for the collective leadership of the church to share with the consultation team and a time for the consultation team to dig deeper into a particular subject that is unclear or needs more conversation. There is no set agenda for this time together. Yet, this time with the leaders has always resulted in being some of the most valuable time set aside for the consultation team and leaders. This lasts an hour and is normally scheduled from 9:00 to 10:00 a.m.

## Congregational Teaching Time

From approximately 10:00 a.m. until 3:00 p.m., the congregation will come together for dreaming, conversation, sharing, and teaching by your consultant. There are exercises conducted by small groups at tables as part of the time together. The purpose of the day is to learn how to reach more people and be a competent, compelling congregation faithful in the mission. It is also a time for the consultant to share what they have heard and learned throughout the process. This presentation is available on the HCI website.

## Congregation's Recommended Next Steps

The last hour of the day will be spent creating next steps. Based on what was learned and heard, the consultant will lead the workshop participants in creating action steps. This will be done in groups at tables and shared with the group at large. At the conclusion of the workshop, the small-group recommendations will be gathered by the leadership team (board/council). The leadership team will meet in the upcoming week or two and decide which action steps to adopt for implementation.

Another option is for the consultation team to identify congregation strengths and concerns and write "prescriptions" on how to address the concerns. Yet another option |is for both the small groups in the Saturday workshop and the consultation team to write recommendations. This allows the leadership team to gauge their recommendations for congregation action steps on both the outside perspective and the inside perspective.

## *Discernment Time*

Whether your congregation decides to write their own action steps, have the consultation team write their action steps, or both, it is imperative to spend some time communicating, discerning, and praying. The time and method needed for this discernment will depend greatly on which pathway you choose for action steps/recommendations and your church's polity. While correct procedure needs to be followed for your local and denominational requirements, please do not miss the biggest opportunity for seeking God's will. What is it that God is calling your church to be and become? This is a heart and soul decision. This is not a head decision. Ask your congregation to be in prayer for this discernment. Provide opportunities for your congregation to come together to ask questions to understand the recommendations the church is considering to become a more faithful, competent, and compelling congregation. Spend time praying together.

## *Leadership Adopts a Plan*

Approximately thirty days after the Dream Weekend, either the congregation will vote on the recommendations or the board/council will roll out the recommendations, depending on which pathway was chosen (and your church polity) going into the Dream Weekend. Once the recommendations are adopted, you are ready to move into the implementation phase in section 5.

# Section 4 Discussion Questions

## *Outside Help*

Will you bring in outside help to facilitate the Dream Weekend? If so, whom will you ask? Consultant? Coach? Both (best practice)? Who is responsible for inviting them? What is the budget for doing so? When do you need to start the process of locating them?

Indicate below the decision of the team on hiring outside help, as well as the decisions you have made on the person/people to invite to facilitate, the budget, and when to start this search process. Finally, indicate the person responsible for completing this task.

## *Reminders*

Take a look at the reminders on the checklist below. Many of these items should already be in process, but now is a great time to make sure all the details are covered.

Record below any gaps in the checklist where further work or coordination needs to occur. Indicate the gaps and who is responsible for bridging each gap.

## *Thirty Days*

What is the plan for the thirty days of discernment? Will you conduct gatherings of your congregation for the opportunity to discuss the recommendations/next steps? If so, how many gathering opportunities will you plan? How will those times be communicated to the congregation? Who will conduct those conversations? How will the congregation be invited into prayer and discernment in these thirty days?

Indicate below your church's plan for this thirty-day discernment period.

## *Decision*

How will the decision be made to move forward with the action steps or recommendations? Congregational vote? Leadership vote? When will the decision be made? How will the decision be communicated to the congregation? Does your church polity require an outside person or denominational leaders to conduct a vote?

Indicate below the process your church will use to come to a decision and how it will be communicated.

# Section 4 Checklist

_____ Recruit outside help for best results.

_____ Make the decision of whether you will implement congregational recommendations or consultation team prescriptions.

_____ Set the date for the Dream Weekend and communicate with the congregation.

_____ Work on the interview schedule for the Dream Weekend.

_____ Recruit the focus group.

_____ Plan for meals, hospitality, and childcare for the Dream Weekend.

_____ Overcommunicate about the need for everyone's participation in the Dream Weekend.

_____ Host the Dream Weekend.

_____ Conduct congregational conversations about the recommendations.

_____ Set aside thirty days for prayer and discernment.

_____ Adopt recommendations or prescriptions.

_____ Move to the implementation stage.

**R**

# Implementation and Coaching

## Implementation

This is again a critical juncture in your transformation process, and this part also needs some outside help. While some of the recommendations can be implemented with the resources on hand, you will probably have a significant need for some outside help. For if your church knew they needed to implement something and knew how to do it, they would have most likely already done it! The implementation needs to be started right away. It will most likely start with the forming of teams to learn, create, and implement various processes, new ministries, and so on. The outside help can come from a variety of resources including a coach, consultant, or person within a given area of specialty (e.g., facilities or worship). Just make sure the person you bring in understands how their part ties into the overall process and mission. (See under the Resources tab on the HCI website for possible resources for implementation.)

The implementation will probably take place over eighteen to twenty-four months. Implementation is usually loaded on the front end with assembling people and getting the implementation process started. The latter end of the implementation process is typically slower as you move into the more adaptive changes and larger projects. It is really easy to lose momentum and motivation after the first year. But know that this is where the real transformation begins. Don't stop at this pivotal time when the hard work will just be beginning to pay off.

Please don't treat the recommendations as a to-do list. If you do, your church will not realize the transformation that is possible. Transformation is hard work. It is layered work. If you only *do* the work but do not live into a different way of *being* a church, you will lose sight of this being a process and the reasons you are doing it. You have to live into the essence of the prescriptions not just do the prescriptions. For example, if you only write a vision statement, but never start gauging the life of your congregation on living into the vision, you have done nothing more than write a story. When you live into the vision, you are creating a new story for your congregation. That is, you have created a new way of doing church that creates a body of Christ that is more competent and compelling by reaching people in culturally relevant ways.

Continue to have your prayer team praying for the process, the pastor, the leaders, and the community. Prayer works! Keep it coming!

# Follow-Up and Accountability

The board/council must hold the pastor accountable. The pastor must hold the teams accountable for the implementation of the prescriptions. For if there is not accountability, there will likely be no transformation. For example, each board/council meeting should be primarily spent on talking about the progress of the recommendations as reported by the pastor. If progress is not on schedule, the board/council needs to be asking about ways to support the pastor in accomplishing the recommendations, what the obstacles are, and how they can be helpful. There must be a consistent follow-up process with accountability to make sure progress is occurring and nothing is falling through the cracks.

The congregation must have opportunities to hear about the progress of the recommendations and ask questions. Remember, transparency is vitally important in the life of a competent and compelling congregation. This is a great time to practice transparency by holding quarterly congregational conversations to share progress and answer questions.

# Coaching

We highly recommend hiring a coach to help with your implementation. The coach provides an outside eye and voice as well as someone outside the congregation to ask the hard questions and keep everyone accountable for the benchmarks and completion of the recommendations. The coach is also a great resource for information and teaching. The coach becomes a partner in the transformation process. The coach typically works with the pastor and congregation monthly during the eighteen to twenty-four months of implementation. The coach asks the harder questions that are typically difficult to ask one another within the congregation. The coach stretches the pastor and leaders to implement at a deeper, more adaptive level. The coach is the one that can hold the mirror up for the pastor, leaders, and congregation to reflect the current reality. The coach champions, encourages, and motivates the congregation when the going gets tough. The coach is an invaluable member of the transformation team of the church. Strongly consider investing in a coach who has experience and specializes in congregational transformation. Check out the Our Team tab on the HCI website for coaches experienced in this process.

# Never Finished

As much as we would like to be finished, the transformation process is never complete. If we stay stagnate for any amount of time, our churches will become irrelevant in our mission fields. We must be in a constant state of evaluation. We must continuously strive toward excellence. We must continuously evaluate our progress on our mission and vision. We must continuously work toward being the best stewards of our resources. Remember this is a process, not a program. This process is designed to create an everlasting organization that continuously strives toward being faithful to God for reaching people in this broken world. That work, my friends, is never finished. Press on, faithful followers. Press on!

# Section 5 Discussion Questions

## *Accountability*

How will your church leaders be accountable for moving the process forward? Who and what processes need to be in place to ensure this occurs?

Describe below your accountability process and who is responsible.

## *Coach*

If your church has not already hired a coach who is familiar with his process, will you now hire one? What expectations do you have of the coach? What qualifications and experience do you desire? How will you recruit a coach? Who is responsible for the recruitment? What is the church budget for a coach?

Indicate below your decision on coaching. If you are hiring a coach, record who is responsible for doing so, the expectations, and the budget.

## *Other Resources*

In reviewing your actions steps or recommendations, what other resources are needed to complete them. Materials? Experts? How will you find these resources? Who is responsible for finding them?

As a vision team, review the recommendations together and decide where additional resources are needed. Indicate the gaps below, what resources are needed, and who is responsible for bridging the gaps.

# *Keep Going*

Whether you are in the midst of implementation or at its completion, remember that it is never finished. How do you create a culture of continuous evaluation toward becoming an ever more competent and compelling congregation that reaches new people?

As a vision team, discuss how to create the culture of continuous evaluation. Write a plan below of how the church will live into this culture and how the vision team and other leaders will create opportunities for this evaluation.

# Section 5 Checklist

_____ Create a system for accountability.

_____ Provide opportunities for congregational conversation.

_____ Hire a coach as a best practice.

_____ Continue to be in prayer for the process and your mission field.

_____ Don't give up! Keep going! Transformation is hard, but so worth it!

_____ When implementation is complete, start again. What are the next recommendations that would lead your congregation to be more competent and compelling?

CPSIA information can be obtained at www.ICGtesting.com
Printed in the USA
LVOW03s1924080415

433642LV00002B/2/P

9 781630 885755